# 200 + Frequently Asked Interview Q & A in SQL, PL/SQL,

# Database Development & Administration

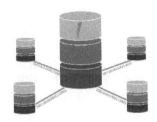

By Bandana Ojha

# Introduction

"The book 200 + Frequently Asked Interview Q & A in SQL , PL/SQL,

Database Development & Administration " contains SQL/PL SQL/ Database interview notes with simple and straightforward explanations. Rather than going through comprehensive, textbook-sized reference guides, this book contains only the information required for interview to start their career as database developer or database administrator. Answers of all the questions are short and to the point. This book contains 200+ questions and answers and we assure that you will get 90% frequently asked  interview questions in SQL /PL SQL/DBD and DBA. This book will clear your fundamentals, concepts and boost your confidence to appear any interview in any companies anywhere in the world whether it is telephonic or face to face. It covers data manipulation queries ,sub queries, procedure, constrains, index, relationships modeling, aggregation, sorting, table joins, DBMS,RDMS and many more.

Check out our other interview  Q & A series. Like Interview Questions & Answers in Manual Testing, Selenium Testing, Mobile Testing, Core Java programming, Advance Java programming, J2EE programming, Python programming, Swift programming ,Scala programming iOS development, Android development and many more.

## 1. What is Collation?

Collation refers to a set of rules that determine how data is sorted and compared. Character data is sorted using rules that define the correct character sequence, with options for specifying case-sensitivity, accent marks, character types and character width.

## 2. What is data visualization?

Data visualization refers to the techniques used to communicate data or information by encoding it as visual objects (e.g. points, lines or bars) contained in graphics.

## 3.What is Referential Integrity?

Set of rules that restrict the values of one or more columns of the tables based on the values of the primary key or unique key of the referenced table.

## 4. What is a data model?

It is a collection of concepts that can be used to describe the structure of a database. It provides necessary means to achieve this abstraction. By structure of a database we mean the data types, relations, and constraints that should hold on the data.

## 5. What is lock escalation?

Lock escalation is used to convert row locks and page locks into table locks thereby "escalating" the smaller or finer locks. This increases the system performance as each lock is nothing but a memory structure. Too many locks would mean more consumption of memory. Hence, escalation is used.

Lock escalation from SQL Server 7.0 onwards is dynamically managed by SQL Server. It is the process of converting a lot of low-level locks into higher level locks.

*6. What is Pivot Table?*

A pivot table is better at the time of grouping. We can also show pivot table like a cross table which is a beneficial feature. But there is one disadvantage of it which is if we must sort a pivot table than we must sort it first according to the first dimension then to the next.

*7. How many types of Privileges are available in SQL?*

There are two types of privileges used in SQL, such as

*System Privilege*: System privileges deal with an object of a particular type and specifies the right to perform one or more actions on it which include Admin allows a user to perform administrative tasks, ALTER ANY INDEX, ALTER ANY CACHE GROUP CREATE/ALTER/DELETE TABLE, CREATE/ALTER/DELETE VIEW etc.

*Object Privilege:* This allows to perform actions on an object or object of another user(s) viz. table, view, indexes etc. Some of the object privileges are EXECUTE, INSERT, UPDATE, DELETE, SELECT, FLUSH, LOAD, INDEX, REFERENCES etc.

## 8. What is the difference between clustered and a non-clustered index?

A clustered index is a special type of index that reorders the way records in the table are physically stored. Therefore, table can have only one clustered index. The leaf nodes of a clustered index contain the data pages.

A nonclustered index is a special type of index in which the logical order of the index does not match the physical stored order of the rows on disk. The leaf node of a nonclustered index does not consist of the data pages. Instead, the leaf nodes contain index rows.

## 9. What is the difference between a local and a global variable?

A Local temporary table exists only for the duration of a connection or, if defined inside a compound statement, for the duration of the compound statement.

A Global temporary table remains in the database permanently, but the rows exist only within a given connection. When connection is closed, the data in the global temporary table disappears. However, the table definition remains with the database for access when database is opened next time.

*10. Explain the levels of data abstraction?*

There are three levels of abstraction :

Physical level :

The lowest level of abstraction describes how data are stored.

Logical level:

The next higher level of abstraction describes what data are stored in database and what relationship among those data.

View level:

The highest level of abstraction describes only part of entire database.

*11. What is the difference between referenced object and dependent object?*

If the definition of an object A references object B, then A is the dependent object and B is the referenced object. If a table is being queried in a procedure, then the table is the referenced object and the procedure is the dependent object. However, if the definition of the table is modified, the procedure may or may not execute correctly.

*12. What is dynamic SQL and what is its usage?*

Dynamic SQL is used by PL/SQL to execute Data Definition Language (DDL) statements, Data Control (DCL) statements, or Transaction Control statements within PL/SQL blocks. These statements are not stored within the source code but are stored as character variables in the program. The SQL statements are created dynamically at runtime by using variables. This is used either using native dynamic SQL or through the DBMS_SQL package.

*13. What is an attribute?*

An entity is represented by a set of attributes.

Attributes are descriptive properties possessed by each member of an entity set.

There are different types of attributes.

Simple

Composite

Single-valued

Derived

## 14. What is an Index?

An index is used to speed up the performance of queries. It makes faster retrieval of data from the table. The index can be created on one column or a group of columns.

## 15. What is @@ERROR?

The @@ERROR automatic variable returns the error code of the last Transact-SQL statement. If there were no error, @@ERROR returns zero. Because @@ERROR is reset after each Transact-SQL statement, it must be saved to a variable if it is needed to process it further after checking it.

## 16. What is an integrity constrains?

An integrity constraint is a declarative way to define a business rule for a column of a table.

## 17. What is log shipping?

Log shipping is the process of automating the backup of database and transaction log files on a production SQL server, and then restoring them onto a standby server. Enterprise Editions only supports log shipping. In log shipping the transactional log file from one server is automatically updated into the backup database on the other server. If one server fails, the other server will have the same db can be used this as the Disaster Recovery plan. The key feature of log shipping is that it will automatically backup transaction logs throughout the day and automatically restore them on the standby server at defined interval.

*18. What is data Integrity?*

Data Integrity defines the accuracy and consistency of data stored in a database. It can also define integrity constraints to enforce business rules on the data when it is entered into the application or database.

*19. What is data mining?*

Data mining refers to using variety of techniques to identify nuggets of information or decision-making knowledge in bodies of data and extracting these in such a way that they can be put in the use in the areas such as decision support, predication, forecasting and estimation.

*20. Define synthetic key?*

Synthetic key is the key where two or more tables consists more than one common column between them is called as synthetic key.

*21. What are nested triggers?*

Triggers may implement data modification logic by using INSERT, UPDATE, and DELETE statement. These triggers that contain data modification logic and find other triggers for data modification are called Nested Triggers.

*22. Why do we use SQL constraints?*

Constraints are used to set the rules for all records in the table. If any constraints get violated, then it can abort the action that caused it.

Constraints are defined while creating the database itself with CREATE TABLE statement or even after the table is created once with ALTER TABLE statement.

*23. Which constraints we can use while creating database in SQL?*

There are 5 major constraints are used in SQL, such as

- NOT NULL: That indicates that the column must have some value and cannot be left null

- UNIQUE: This constraint is used to ensure that each row and column has unique value and no value is being repeated in any other row or column

- PRIMARY KEY: This constraint is used in association with NOT NULL and UNIQUE constraints such as on one or the combination of more than one column to identify the particular record with a unique identity.

- FOREIGN KEY: It is used to ensure the referential integrity of data in the table and also matches the value in one table with another using Primary Key

- CHECK: It is used to ensure whether the value in columns fulfills the specified condition

## 24. What is SQL Injection?

SQL Injection is a type of database attack technique where malicious SQL statements are inserted into an entry field of database such that once it is executed the database is opened for an attacker. This technique is usually used for attacking Data-Driven Applications to have access to sensitive data and perform administrative tasks on databases.

*25. What is case function?*

Case facilitates if-then-else type of logic in SQL. It evaluates a list of conditions and returns one of multiple possible result expressions.

*26. What is Index?*

An index is a physical structure containing pointers to the data. Indices are created in an existing table to locate rows more quickly and efficiently. It is possible to create an index on one or more columns of a table, and each index is given a name. The users cannot see the indexes, they are just used to speed

up queries. Effective indexes are one of the best ways to improve performance in a database application.

*27. What is SQL server agent?*

SQL Server agent plays an important role in the day-to-day tasks of a database administrator (DBA). It is often overlooked as one of the main tools for SQL Server management. Its purpose is to ease the implementation of tasks for the DBA, with its full-function scheduling engine, which allows you to schedule your own jobs and scripts.

## 28. What is concatenation?

It means sequence of interconnected things i.e. any column or row which is related to each other can be connected through concatenation.

## 29. What is  NoConcatenation?

NoConcatenation prefix is used to force the identical tables as two separate internal tables.

## 30. What is a Linked Server?

Linked Servers is a concept in SQL Server by which we can add other SQL Server to a Group and query both the SQL Server dbs using T-SQL Statements. With a linked server, you can create very clean, easy to follow, SQL statements that allow remote data to be retrieved, joined and combined with local data.

## 31. What is a DB trigger?

A DB trigger is a code or programs that automatically execute with response to some event on a table or view in a database. Triggers are created to enforce integrity rules in a database. A trigger is executed every time a data-modification operation occurs (i.e., insert, update or delete).

Triggers are executed automatically on occurrence of one of the data-modification operations.

*32. What is the difference in execution of triggers and stored procedures?*

-The main difference between database trigger and stored procedure is that the trigger is invoked implicitly, and stored procedure is invoked explicitly.

-Transaction Control statements, such as COMMIT, ROLLBACK, and SAVEPOINT, are not allowed within the body of a trigger; whereas, these statements can be included in a stored procedure.

*33.What are the uses of triggers?*

Basically, triggers are used to create consistencies, access restriction and implement securities to the database. Triggers are also used for –

Creating validation mechanisms involving searches in multiple tables

Creating logs to register the use of a table

Update other tables because of inclusion or changes in the current table.

## 34. What is a mutating table?

A mutating table is a table, which is in the state of transition. In other words, it is a table, which is being updated at the time of triggering action. If the trigger code queries this table, then a mutating table error occurs, which causes the trigger to view the inconsistent data.

## 35.How can the performance of a trigger be improved?

The performance of a trigger can be improved by using column names along with the UPDATE clause in the trigger. This will make the trigger fire when that column is updated and therefore, prevents unnecessary action of trigger when other columns are being updated.

## 36. What is schema-level trigger?

Schema-level triggers are created on schema-level operations, such as create table, alter table, drop table, rename, truncate, and revoke. These triggers prevent DDL statements, provide security, and monitor the DDL operations.

## 37. What is the meaning of disabling a trigger?

When a trigger is disabled, it does not mean that it is deleted. The code of the trigger is still stored in the data dictionary, but the trigger will not have any effect on the table.

*38. Do triggers have restrictions on the usage of large datatypes, such as long and long raw?*

Triggers have restrictions on the usage of large datatypes as they cannot declare or reference the LONG and LONG RAW datatypes and cannot use them even if they form part of the object with which the trigger is associated. Similarly, triggers cannot modify the CLOB and BLOB objects as well; however, they can reference them for read-only access.

*39. Can triggers reference other tables through a role?*

Triggers may require referencing other tables while triggering an event. Therefore, privileges required to reference other tables must be granted directly to the owner of the trigger, as the trigger cannot reference other user tables through roles.

*40. Which command is used to delete a trigger?*

DROP TRIGGER command is used to delete a trigger.

## 41. What is the purpose of %type data type?

It assigns a variable the same data type used by the column, for which the variable is created.

## 42. What is a database event trigger?

Trigger that is executed when a database event, such as startup, shutdown, or error, occurs is called a database event trigger. It can be used to reference the attributes of the event and perform system maintenance functions immediately after the database startup.

## 43. How can two pl/sql records be compared?

Two records can be compared by using the equality (comparison) operator for each field of the record. However, the entire record cannot be compared.

## 44. What is a call statement?

A CALL statement within a trigger enables you to call a stored procedure within the trigger rather than writing the Procedural Language/Structured Query Language (PL/SQL) code in it, the procedure may be in PL/SQL, C, or Java language.

## 45. What are SQL constraints?

SQL constraints are the set of rules that enforced some restriction while inserting, deleting or updating of data in the databases.

*46. What are the constraints available in SQL?*

Some of the constraints in SQL are – Primary Key, Foreign Key, Unique Key, SQL Not Null, Default, Check and Index constraint.

*47. What is a unique constraint?*

A unique constraint is used to ensure that there are no duplication values in the field/column.

*48. What is a not null constraint?*

NOT NULL constraint is used to ensure that the value in the filed cannot be a NULL

*49. What is a foreign key?*

A foreign key is used for enforcing referential integrity in which a field marked as foreign key in one table is linked with primary key of another table. With this referential integrity we can have only the data in foreign key which matches the data in the primary key of the other table.

*50. What is the difference between primary key and unique constraints?*

Primary key cannot have NULL value, the unique constraints can have NULL values. There is only one primary key in a table, but there can be multiple unique constrains. The primary key creates the cluster index automatically, but the Unique key does not.

### 51. What is a CHECK constraint?

A CHECK constraint is used to limit the value that is accepted by one or more columns.

### 52. What is Self-Join?

Self-join is set to be query used to compare to itself. This is used to compare values in a column with other values in the same column in the same table. ALIAS ES can be used for the same table comparison.

### 53. What is Cross-Join?

Cross join defines as Cartesian product where number of rows in the first table multiplied by number of rows in the second table. If suppose, WHERE clause is used in cross join then the query will work like an INNER JOIN.

### 54. What is the difference between cross join and full outer join?

A cross join returns cartesian product of the two tables, so there is no condition or on clause as each row of tabelA is joined with each row of tableB whereas a full outer join will join the two tables based on condition specified in the on clause and for the records not satisfying the condition null value is placed in the join result.

*55.* List the different type of joins?

There are various types of joins which are used to retrieve data between the tables. There are four types of joins, namely:

Left Join: Left Join in MySQL is used to return all the rows from the left table but only the matching rows from the right table where the join condition is fulfilled.

Right Join: Right Join in MySQL is used to return all the rows from the right table but only the matching rows from the left table where the join condition is fulfilled.

Full Join: Full join returns all the records when there is a match in any of the tables. Therefore, it returns all the rows from the left-hand side table and all the rows from the right-hand side table.

*56.Differentiate between keep and joins?*

Keep and joins do the same functions but in keep creates the two tables whereas join only creates the one table. Keep is used before the load or select statements.

## 57. What is Equi Join?

Equi Join is a join in which the join comparison operator is an equality. When two tables are joined together using equality or values in one or more columns, they make an Equi Join.

## 58. What is Cartesian Join?

Joining two tables without a where clause produces a Cartesian join which combines every row in one table with every row in another table.

## 59. What is the difference between cross joins and natural joins?

The cross join produces the cross product or Cartesian product of two tables. The natural join is based on all the columns having same name and data types in both the tables.

## 60. What is the Cartesian product of table?

The output of Cross Join is called as a Cartesian product. It returns rows combining each row from the first table with each row of the second table. For Example, if we join two tables having 10 and

20 columns the Cartesian product of two tables will be 10×20=200 Rows.

## 61. What is a Database?

A database is a collection of information in an organized form for faster and better access, storage and manipulation. It can also be defined as a collection of tables, schema, views and other database objects.

## 62. What is Database Testing?

Database testing involves in verifying the integrity of data in the front end with the data present in the back end. It validates the schema, database tables, columns, indexes, stored procedures, triggers, data duplication, orphan records, junk records. It involves in updating records in a database and verifying the same on the front end.

## 63. What is AICD in database?

ACID (an acronym for Atomicity, Consistency Isolation, Durability) is a concept that Database Professionals generally look for when evaluating databases and application architectures. For a reliable database all these four attributes should be achieved.

Atomicity is an all-or-none proposition.

Consistency guarantees that a transaction never leaves your database in a half-finished state.

Isolation keeps transactions separated from each other until they're finished.

Durability guarantees that the database will keep track of pending changes in such a way that the server can recover from an abnormal termination.

### 64. What is DBMS?

A Database Management System (DBMS) is a program that controls creation, maintenance and use of a database. DBMS can be termed as File Manager that manages data in a database rather than saving it in file systems.

### 65. What is RDBMS?

RDBMS stands for Relational Database Management System. RDBMS store the data into the collection of tables, which is related by common fields between the columns of the table. It also provides relational operators to manipulate the data stored into the tables.

### 66. What is the difference between DBMS and RDBMS?

The primary difference between DBMS and RDBMS is, in RDBMS we have relations between the tables of the database. Whereas in DBMS there is no relation between the tables(data may even be stored in files).

RDBMS has primary keys and data is stored in tables. DBMS has no concept of primary keys with data stored in navigational or hierarchical form.

RDBMS defines integrity constraints to follow ACID properties. While DBMS doesn't follow ACID properties.

*67. What is Database White Box Testing?*

Database White Box Testing involves

Database Consistency and ACID properties

Database triggers and logical views

Decision Coverage, Condition Coverage, and Statement Coverage

Database Tables, Data Model, and Database Schema

Referential integrity rules

*68. What is Database Black Box Testing?*

Database Black Box Testing involves

Data Mapping

Data stored and retrieved

Use of Black Box techniques such as Equivalence Partitioning and Boundary Value Analysis (BVA)

## 69. Explain interval match?

The internal match is prefixes with the load statement which is used for connecting different numeric values to one or more numeric interval.

## 70. Explain internal match function()?

Internal match function is used to generate data bucket of different sizes.

## 71. What do you understand by extended interval match function()?

Extended interval match function() is used for slowly changing the dimensions.

## 72.What is Container?

A container object is used to keep multiple charts. We can use a container object to keep many charts in the same box.

## 73. What are the PL/SQL cursors?

Oracle uses workspaces to execute the SQL commands. In other words, when Oracle processes a SQL command, it opens an area in the memory called Private SQL Area. A cursor is an identifier for this area. It allows programmers to name this area and access its information.

*74. How Cursors work?*

Cursor follows steps as given below

Declare Cursor

Open Cursor

Retrieve row from the Cursor

Process the row

Close Cursor

Deallocate Cursor

*75. When is the Explicit Cursor Used ?*

If the developer needs to perform the row by row operations for the result set containing more than one row, then he unambiguously declares a pointer with a name. They are managed by OPEN, FETCH and CLOSE.%FOUND, %NOFOUND, %ROWCOUNT and %ISOPEN characteristics are used in all types of pointers.

*76. What is the difference between implicit cursor and explicit cursor?*

A cursor is a SQL memory work area. Any SQL statement always uses a cursor for the execution of statements and fetching of results. This is implicitly defined and is called implicit cursor.

When a programmer defines a cursor for fetching and parsing results of a SQL query, which returns more than one row, it is called an explicit cursor.

## 77. What is the difference between Local and Global temporary table?

If defined in inside a compound statement a local temporary table exists only for the duration of that statement, but a global temporary table exists permanently in the DB, but its rows disappear when the connection is closed.

## 78. What is the difference between unique key and primary key?

A unique key allows null value(although only one) but a primary key doesn't allow null values. A table can have more than one unique key columns while there can be only one primary key. A unique key column creates non-clustered index whereas primary key creates a clustered index on the column.

## 79. What are transactions in SQL?

Transaction is a set of operations performed in a logical sequence. It is executed, if any statement in the transaction fails, the whole transaction is marked as failed and not committed to the database.

*80. What are the different types of locks in database?*

The different types of locks in database are-

Shared locks – Allows data to be read-only(Select operations), prevents the data to be updated when in shared lock.

Update locks – Applied to resources that can be updated. There can be only one update lock on a data at a time.

Exclusive locks – Used to lock data being modified(INSERT, UPDATE, or DELETE) by one transaction thus ensuring that multiple updates cannot be made to the same resource at the same time.

Intent locks – A notification mechanism using which a transaction conveys that intends to acquire lock on data.

Schema locks- Used for operations when schema or structure of the database is required to be updated.

Bulk Update locks – Used in case of bulk operations when the TABLOCK hint is used.

81.*What are Scalar Functions in SQL?*

Scalar Functions are used to return a single value based on the input values. Scalar Functions are as follows

UCASE(): Converts the specified field in upper case

LCASE(): Converts the specified field in lower case

MID(): Extracts and returns character from text field

FORMAT(): Specifies the display format

LEN(): Specifies the length of text field

ROUND(): Rounds up the decimal field value to a number

82. *What is the difference between a HAVING CLAUSE and a WHERE CLAUSE?*

Specifies a search condition for a group or an aggregate. HAVING can be used only with the SELECT

statement. HAVING is typically used in a GROUP BY clause. When GROUP BY is not used, HAVING behaves like a WHERE clause. Having Clause is basically used only with the GROUP BY function in a

query. WHERE Clause is applied to each row before they are part of the GROUP BY function in a query.

### 83. What is subquery?

A subquery is a query within another query. The outer query is called as main query, and inner query is called subquery. Subquery is always executed first, and the result of subquery is passed on to the main query.

### 84. What are the different types of a subquery?

There are two types of subquery namely, Correlated and Non-Correlated.

Correlated subquery: These are queries which select the data from a table referenced in the outer query. It is not considered as an independent query as it refers to another table and refers the column in a table.

Non-Correlated subquery: This query is an independent query where the output of subquery is substituted in the main query.

## 85. What is difference between Co-related sub query and nested sub query?

Correlated subquery runs once for each row selected by the outer query. It contains a reference to a value from the row selected by the outer query.

Nested subquery runs only once for the entire nesting (outer) query. It does not contain any reference to the outer query row.

## 86. How many row comparison operators are used while working with a subquery?

There are 3-row comparison operators which are used in subqueries such as IN, ANY and ALL.

## 87. What is the use of optimized load?

Optimized load is much faster and preferable especially for large set of data. It is possible if no transformation is made at the time of load and no filtering is done.

## 88. What are different type of Collation Sensitivity?

The different phases of transaction are

Case sensitivity

Accent sensitivity

Kana Sensitivity

Width sensitivity

*89. What is a Relationship and what are they?*

Relation or links are between entities that have something to do with each other. Relationships are defined as the connection between the tables in a database. There are various relationships, namely:

One to One Relationship.

One to Many Relationship.

Many to One Relationship.

Self-Referencing Relationship.

*90. How many types of Privileges are available in SQL?*

There are two types of privileges used in SQL, such as

System Privilege: System privileges deal with an object of a particular type and specifies the right to perform one or more actions on it which include Admin allows a user to perform administrative tasks, ALTER ANY INDEX, ALTER ANY CACHE GROUP CREATE/ALTER/DELETE TABLE, CREATE/ALTER/DELETE VIEW etc.

Object Privilege: This allows to perform actions on an object or object of another user(s) viz. table, view, indexes etc. Some of the object privileges are EXECUTE, INSERT, UPDATE, DELETE, SELECT, FLUSH, LOAD, INDEX, REFERENCES etc.

## 91. What do you mean by Stored Procedures? How do we use it?

A stored procedure is a collection of SQL statements which can be used as a function to access the database. We can create these stored procedures previously before using it and can execute these them wherever we require and also apply some conditional logic to it. Stored procedures are also used to reduce network traffic and improve the performance.

## 92. What are aggregate functions in SQL?

Aggregate functions are the SQL functions which return a single value calculated from multiple values of columns. Some of the aggregate functions in SQL are-

Count() – Returns the count of the number of rows returned by the SQL expression

Max() – Returns the max value out of the total values

Min() – Returns the min value out of the total values

Avg() – Returns the average of the total values

Sum() – Returns the sum of the values returned by the SQL expression

*93. What is user defined Function?*

User-Defined Functions allow to define its own T-SQL functions that can accept 0 or more parameters and return a single scalar data value or a table data type.

*94. What is the use of NVL function?*

NVL function is used to convert the null value to its actual value.

*95. What are the specific uses of SQL functions?*

SQL functions have the following uses –

Performing calculations on data

Modifying individual data items

Manipulating the output

Formatting dates and numbers

Converting data types

## 95. Which function returns the remainder in a division operation?

The MOD function returns the remainder in a division operation.

## 96. What are DMVs?

Dynamic management views (DMVs) and functions return server state information that can be used to monitor the health of a server instance, diagnose problems, and tune performance; that is, they let you see what is going on inside SQL Server. They were introduced in SQL Server 2005 as an alternative to system tables.

## 97. Explain the difference between a function, procedure and package ?

A function and procedure are the same in that they are intended to be a collection of PL/SQL code that carries a single task. While a procedure does not have to return any values to the calling application, a function will return a single value. A package on the other hand is a collection of functions and procedures that are grouped together based on their commonality to a business function or application.

*98. Can there be multiple return statements within a function?*

Yes, there can be multiple RETURN statements within a function though only one is executed. After the value is retuned, the control passes back to the calling environment and function processing is stopped.

*99. Is it possible to define a return statement in the exception part of a function?*

Yes, it is possible to define RETURN statement in the exception section. This RETURN statement would be executed if an exception is raised and control is passed to the exception section of the code.

*100. What is the basic difference between procedure and function?*

A procedure is executed as a PL/SQL statement. It can accept more than one parameter as an input from the calling environment and may return none, one, or more than one value.

A function is invoked as a part of expression. It can have more than one parameter as an input from the calling environment and it should return a single value to the calling environment using the RETURN statement.

*101. What is a View?*

A view is like a subset of a table which is stored logically in a database. A view is a virtual table. It contains rows and columns like a real table. The fields in the view are fields from one or more real tables. Views do not contain data of their own. They are used to restrict access to the database or to hide data complexity.

*102. What are the advantages of Views?*

Some of the advantages of Views are

Views occupy no space

Views are used to simply retrieve the results of complicated queries that need to be executed often.

Views are used to restrict access to the database or to hide data complexity.

*103. What are the three basic sections of a PL/SQL block?*

Below are the three basic sections of a PL/SQL block

Declaration section

Execution section

Exception section

*104. What is the difference between GUI Testing and Database Testing?*

GUI testing is user interface testing or front-end testing

Database testing is  back-end testing or data testing.

GUI testing deals with all the testable items that are open to the user to interaction such as Menus, Forms etc.

Database testing deals with all the testable items that are generally hidden from the user.

The tester who is performing GUI Testing doesn't need to know Structured Query Language

The tester who is performing Database Testing needs to know Structured Query Language

GUI testing includes invalidating the text boxes, check boxes, buttons, drop-downs, forms etc., majorly the look and feel of the overall application

Database Testing involves in verifying the integrity of data in the front end with the data present in the back end. It validates the schema, database tables, columns, indexes, stored procedures, triggers, data duplication, orphan records, junk records. It involves in updating records in a database and verifying the same on the front end.

*105. What is Normalization and what are the advantages of it?*

Normalization is the process of organizing data to avoid duplication and redundancy. Some of the advantages are:

Better Database organization

More Tables with smaller rows

Efficient data access

Greater Flexibility for Queries

Quickly find the information

Easier to implement Security

Allows easy modification

Reduction of redundant and duplicate data

More Compact Database

Ensure Consistent data after modification

*106.How many Normalization forms are there?*

There are 5 forms of Normalization

First Normal Form (1NF): It removes all duplicate columns from the table. Creates table for related data and identifies unique column values

First Normal Form (2NF): Follows 1NF and creates and places data subsets in an individual table and defines relationship between tables using primary key

Third Normal Form (3NF): Follows 2NF and removes those columns which are not related through primary key

Fourth Normal Form (4NF): Follows 3NF and do not define multi-valued dependencies. 4NF also known as BCNF

*107. What is De-normalization?*

De-normalization is the process of attempting to optimize the performance of a database by adding redundant data. It is sometimes necessary because current DBMSs implement the relational model poorly. A true relational DBMS would allow for a fully normalized database at the logical level, while providing physical storage of data that is tuned for high performance. De-normalization is a technique to move from higher to lower normal forms of database modeling in order to speed up database access.

## 108. What is a query?

A DB query is a code written in order to get the information back from the database. Query can be designed in such a way that it matched with our expectation of the result set. Simply, a question to the Database.

## 109. What is OLTP?

Online Transaction Processing (OLTP) relational databases are optimal for managing changing data. When several users are performing transactions at the same time, OLTP databases are designed to let transactional applications write only the data needed to handle a single transaction as quickly as possible.

## 110. What is RAID?

RAID, an acronym for Redundant Array of Independent Disks (sometimes incorrectly referred to as Redundant Array of Inexpensive Disks), is a technology that provides increased storage functions and reliability through redundancy.

*111. What is the difference between NULL value, Zero, and Blank space?*

Null value is field with no value which is different from zero value and blank space.

Null value is a field with no value.

Zero is a number

Blank space is the value we provide. The ASCII value of space is CHAR(32).

*112. What is the difference between Rename and Alias?*

Rename is a permanent name given to a table or column whereas Alias is a temporary name given to a table or column.

*113. What is BCP? When does it used?*

Bulk Copy is a tool used to copy huge amount of data from tables and views. BCP does not copy the structures same as source to destination.

*114. Define candidate key, alternate key, composite key?*

A candidate key is one that can identify each row of a table uniquely. Generally, a candidate key becomes the primary key of the table.

If the table has more than one candidate key, one of them will become the primary key, and the rest are called alternate keys.

A key formed by combining at least two or more columns is called composite key.

*115. What is a composite primary key?*

Primary key created on more than one column is called composite primary key.

*116. What are the different DML commands in SQL?*

DML commands are used for managing data present in the database.

      SELECT: To select specific data from a database

      INSERT: To insert new records into a table

      UPDATE: To update existing records

      DELETE: To delete existing records from a table

*117. What are the different DCL commands in SQL?*

DCL commands are used to create roles, grant permission and control access to the database objects.

GRANT: To provide user access

DENY: To deny permissions to users

REVOKE: To remove user access

*118. What are the different TCL commands in SQL?*

TCL commands are used to manage the changes made by DML statements.

COMMIT: To write and store the changes to the database

ROLLBACK: To restore the database since the last commit

*119. What is a NULL value?*

A field with a NULL value is a field with no value. A NULL value is different from a zero value or a field that contains spaces. A field with a NULL value is one that has been left blank during record creation. Assume, there is a field in a table is optional and it is possible to insert a record without adding a value to the optional field then the field will be saved with a NULL value.

## 120. What is Built-in/Administrator?

The Built-in/Administrator account is basically used during some setup to join some machine in the domain. It should be disabled immediately thereafter. For any disaster recovery, the account will be automatically enabled. It should not be used for normal operations.

## 121. What is Auto Increment?

Auto increment keyword allows the user to create a unique number to be generated when a new record is inserted into the table. AUTO INCREMENT keyword can be used in Oracle and IDENTITY keyword can be used in SQL SERVER.

## 122. What are the different types of data models ?

Following are the types of data models

Entity relationship model

Relational model

Hierarchical model

Network model

Object oriented model

Object relational model

## 123. What do you mean by flat file database?

It is a database in which there are no programs or user access languages. It has no cross-file capabilities but is user-friendly and provides user-interface management.

*124. What is relational algebra?*

It is procedural query language. It consists of a set of operations that take one or two relations as input and produce a new relation.

*125. How to copy the tables, schema and views from one SQL server to another?*

Microsoft SQL Server 2000 Data Transformation Services (DTS) is a set of graphical tools and programmable objects that lets user extract, transform, and consolidate data from disparate sources into single or multiple destinations.

*126. What is a Catalog?*

A catalog is a table that contain the information such as structure of each file ,the type and storage format of each data item and various constraints on the data. The information stored in the catalog is called Metadata . Whenever a request is made to access a particular data, the DBMS s/w refers to the catalog to determine the structure of the file.

*127. How do you maintain database integrity where deletions from one table will automatically cause deletions in another table?*

You can create a trigger that will automatically delete elements in the second table when elements from the first table are removed.

*128. What is buffer cache?*

Buffer cache is a memory pool in which data pages are read. The ideal performance of the buffer cache is indicated as: 95% indicates that pages that were found in the memory are 95% of time. Another 5% is need physical disk access.

If the value falls below 90%, it is the indication of more physical memory requirement on the server.

*129. What is log Cache?*

Log cache is a memory pool used to read and write the log pages. A set of cache pages are available in each log cache. The synchronization is reduced between log and data buffers by managing log cache separately from the buffer cache.

*130. How to store pdf file in SQL Server?*

Create a column as type 'blob' in a table. Read the content of the file and save in 'blob' type column in a table.

Or

Store them in a folder and establish the pointer to link them in the database.

*131. What is the difference between blob and clob?*

The BLOB datatype is used to store a binary large object, such as a video image file; whereas, the CLOB datatype is used to store a character large object.

*132. What is the difference between to_blob and to_clob functions?*

The TO_CLOB function is used to convert the LONG, VARCHAR2, and CHAR datatypes to the CLOB datatype.

The TO_BLOB function is used to convert the LONG RAW and RAW datatype to the BLOB datatype.

*133. Is it possible to convert clob to char type?*

Yes, it possible to convert CLOB to CHAR type using the TO_CHAR function.

## 134. What is the difference between internal and external lobs?

LOB datatype can be internal or external. Internal LOBs are CLOB, NCLOB, and BLOB that are stored in the database; whereas, external LOBs are BFILEs that are stored outside the database as external files. Although both LOB types have the pointer to the location, the BFILEs are stored externally across hard disks or on external storage; whereas, internal LOBs have to be stored in the different location within the database itself.

## 135. What is a cluster Key?

The related columns of the tables are called the cluster key. The cluster key is indexed using a cluster index and its value is stored only once for multiple tables in the cluster.

## 136. What are defaults?

A default is a value that will be used by a column, if no value is supplied to that column while inserting data. IDENTITY columns and timestamp columns can't have defaults bound to them.

## 137. What is specialization?

It is the process of defining a set of subclasses of an entity type where each subclass contains all the attributes and relationships of the parent entity and may have additional attributes and relationships which are specific to itself.

*138. What are the different subsets of SQL?*

The different subsets of SQL are:

DDL (Data Definition Language): It allows you to perform various operations on the database such as CREATE, ALTER and DELETE objects.

DML ( Data Manipulation Language) – It allows you to access and manipulate data. It helps you to insert, update, delete and retrieve data from the database.

DCL ( Data Control Language) – It allows you to control access to the database. Example – Grant, Revoke access permissions.

*139. What is Straight Table?*

A straight table is much better at the time of sorting as compared to the pivot table as we can sort it according to any column as per our choice.

*140. What are orphan records?*

Orphan records are the records having foreign key to a parent record which doesn't exist or got deleted.

## 141. 110. What is the difference between CHAR and VARCHAR2 datatype in SQL?

Both CHAR and VARCHAR2 are used for characters but varchar2 is used for character strings of variable length whereas char is used for character strings of fixed length.

## 142. What is the difference between DELETE and TRUNCATE statements?

The difference between truncate and delete command are represented in the below table:

DELETE TRUNCATE

Delete command is used to delete a row in a table. Truncate is used to delete all the rows from a table.

You can rollback data after using delete statement. You cannot rollback data.

It is a DML command. It is a DDL command.

It is slower than truncate statement. It is faster.

## 143. Is a null value same as that of zero or a blank space?

A null value is not at all same as that of zero or a blank space. NULL value represents a value which is unavailable, unknown, assigned or not applicable whereas a zero is a number and blank space is a character.

*144. What is the difference between static and dynamic SQL?*

Static SQL is hard-coded in a program when the programmer knows the statements to be executed.

Dynamic SQL the program must dynamically allocate memory to receive the query results.

*145. What are the properties of the Relational tables?*

Relational tables have six properties:

Values are atomic.

Column values are of the same kind.

Each row is unique.

The sequence of columns is insignificant.

The sequence of rows is insignificant.

Each column must have a unique name.

*146. What are the different phases of transaction?*

The different phases of transaction are

Analysis phase

Redo Phase

Undo phase

## 147. What is meant by query optimization?

The phase that identifies an efficient execution plan for evaluating a query that has the least estimated cost is referred to as query optimization.

## 148. What is SQL Profiler?

SQL Profiler is a graphical tool that allows system administrators to monitor events in an instance of Microsoft SQL Server. You can capture and save data about each event to a file or SQL Server table to analyze later.

## 149. What are the risks of storing a hibernate-managed object in cache? How do you overcome the problems?

The primary problem here is that the object will outlive the session it came from. Lazily loaded properties won't get loaded if needed later. To overcome the problem, perform cache on the object's id and class and then retrieve the object in the current session context.

## 150. What is the difference between buffer cache and log cache in SQL Server?

Buffer cache is a memory pool in which data pages are read. The ideal performance of the buffer cache is indicated as: 95% indicates that pages that were found in the memory are 95% of time. Another 5% is need physical disk access. If the value falls below 90%, it is the indication of more physical memory requirement on the server.

Log cache is a memory pool used to read and write the log pages. A set of cache pages are available in each log cache. The synchronization is reduced between log and data buffers by managing log cache separately from the buffer cache.

### 151. What is a CTE?

A common table expression (CTE) is a temporary named result set that can be used within other statements like SELECT, INSERT, UPDATE, and DELETE. It is not stored as an object and its lifetime is limited to the query. It is defined using the WITH statement.

### 152. What is the default port number for SQL Server?

If enabled, the default instance of Microsoft SQL Server listens on TCP port 1433. Named instances are configured for dynamic ports, so an available port is chosen when SQL Server starts. When connecting to a named instance through a firewall, configure the Database Engine to listen on a specific port, so that the appropriate port can be opened in the firewall.

*153. What is the purpose of the MERGE statement in SQL?*

The MERGE statement allows conditional update or insertion of data into a database table. It performs an UPDATE if the rows exist, or an INSERT if the row does not exist.

*154. Which SQL statement is used to add, modify or drop columns in a database table?*

The ALTER TABLE statement is used to add, modify or drop columns in a database table.

*155. What is the default ordering of data using the ORDER BY clause? How could it be changed?*

The default sorting order is ascending. It can be changed using the DESC keyword, after the column name in the ORDER BY clause.

*156. What is the purpose of the condition operators BETWEEN and IN?*

The BETWEEN operator displays rows based on a range of values. The IN condition operator checks for values contained in a specific set of values.

*157. How do you declare a user-defined exception?*

User defined exceptions are declared under the DECLARE section, with the keyword EXCEPTION. Syntax –

<exception_name> EXCEPTION;

*158.What is the purpose of %rowtype data type?*

It declares a composed variable that is equivalent to the row of a table. After the variable is created, the fields of the table can be accessed, using the name of this variable.

*159. What are transaction control statements? Can they be used within the PL/SQL block?*

Transaction Control statements are the COMMIT and REVOKE commands that control the logic of transactions within a database. These statements are valid within a PL/SQL block. The COMMIT command terminates the active transaction and makes the changes permanent to the database. The ROLLBACK command terminates the active transaction but cancels any changes that were made to the database.

## 160. What is an anonymous block?

Any PL/SQL block, which does not have a name, is called an anonymous block. It is directly written in the application code and compiled by the PL/SQL engine at the time of execution.

## 161. What is schema?

A schema is a collection of database objects of a user.

## 162. What is indirect reference of schema objects?

When any procedure or function references another schema object through an intermediate procedure, function, or view, then the reference is called indirect reference.

## 163. Name few schema objects that can be created using PL/SQL?

Stored procedures and functions

Packages

Triggers

Cursors

## 164. What is star schema?

The simplest form of dimensional model, in which data is prearranged into facts and dimensions is known as Star schema.

*165. What is Snowflake Schema?*

A snowflake schema is a difference of the star schema. Snowflake is used to improve the presentation of a particular queries.

*166. What are the difference between a data block, an extent and a segment ?*

A data block is the smallest unit of logical storage for a database object. As objects grow they take chunks of additional storage that are composed of contiguous data blocks. These groupings of contiguous data blocks are called extents. All the extents that an object takes when grouped together are considered the segment of the database object.

*167. What is a package and how does it differ from procedure and function?*

A package is a group of logically related PL/SQL subprograms bundled together with PL/SQL types and other associated objects. It consists of the following two parts:

Package specification —Includes declaration of all the objects and subprograms that are part of the package.

Package body—Includes the total definition of all the parts of a package that have been declared in the specification.

The whole package is fully loaded into the memory when any package construct is called for the first time. Therefore, it does not require any disk input/output on later calls to constructs in the same package.

*168. What is the difference between private package construct and public package construct?*

-Public package constructs are declared in the package specification but defined in the package body and can be invoked from any other object in the oracle environment.

-Private package constructs are those that are declared and defined only within the package body. They are not declared in the package specification and can only be referenced by other constructs, which are part of the same package.

-Private package construct is always defined before a public package construct within the package body.

## 169. Can a complete package be called?

No, a complete package is not possible to call, invoke, or parameterize; however, any construct from the package can be called or invoked.

## 170. What is the difference between local and global variables within a package?

A local variable is defined within a package body and is only available to the constructs within the same package.

A global variable is one that is declared in the package specification. This can be referenced outside the package and is visible, to external objects that have access privilege on the package.

## 171. Is it possible to write a package specification without a package body?

Yes, it is possible to write a package specification without a package body but not the vice versa. This is specifically used if there is a package, which is only used for the declaration of public variables, types, constants, and exceptions. In such case, there is no need for a package body and only package specification is enough.

*172. What is written as part of the package specification and the package body?*

The package specification consists of the declaration of all the global variables, cursors, types, procedures, and functions that are public and required to be called from within or outside the package.

The package body consists of the definition of all the public constructs that are declared within the package specification and the definition of all the private variables, cursors, types, procedures, and functions that are required only within the package.

*173. What are the advantages of using packages?*

The main advantages of using packages are given as follows:

Encapsulation —Packages provide encapsulation of all the logically related constructs together in a single module, which is easy to code and understand.

Better application design —Both modularity and encapsulation leads to better designing of applications. Separate package specification and body helps in simplifying the coding and better definition of the subprograms.

Hiding —Public and private constructs can be defined and declared so that any definition can be hidden to protect integrity of the package. Any changes in the private constructs only need the package body to be recompiled without the need for the entire application to be recompiled.

Better performance —A call to any construct within the package loads the entire package in the memory; therefore, enables better performance of the application.

*174.How do you refer to the types, objects and subprograms declared within a package?*

The types, objects, and subprograms declared within a package are referred to using the dot notation as –

package_name.type_name

package_name.object_name

package_name.subprogram_name

*175. How does a package support information hiding?*

A package consists of two parts: package specification and package body. The package specification contains the names of procedures and functions, their parameters, and return types; whereas, the subprogram code is part of the package body. Developers who require calling the procedures or functions just need to have access on the package specification. Therefore, the package owner can grant privilege on the package specification while hiding the package body. In this way, the developers can use the package without seeing the actual code. In addition, package owners can create procedures and functions that are private for the package and need not be part of the package specification. In this way, information hiding is achieved within a package.

*176. Where can a package be stored?*

A package can be stored on the server side within a schema in the database. It can also be stored on the client side in the form of Oracle Reports, Oracle Forms, or as part of PL/SQL library.

*177. What is an exception?*

An exception is an identifier, which defines an error condition within the Procedural

Language/Structured Query Language (PL/SQL) code. When an error occurs, it is trapped, and the program control unconditionally branches to the exception section of the PL/SQL block.

*178. What is the difference between a temporary tablespace and a permanent tablespace?*

A temporary tablespace is used for temporary objects such as sort structures while permanent tablespaces are used to store those objects meant to be used as the true objects of the database.

*179. How is global variable declared within a nested block?*

Any variable declared within a block is local to the block and global to the nested blocks. The variables declared within the nested blocks are unknown to the outer blocks. They override the references to any outer declared variables with the same name unless they are used with the block label name.

*180. What is the difference between nested tables and VARRAYs?*

Both nested tables and VARRAYs are collection types that can be stored in the database. They differ in two properties, bounding and sparsity. Bounding refers to the limit on the number of elements that a collection can have; whereas, sparsity means whether there can be gaps within the subscripts or not.

Nested tables are not bounded and can be sparse; whereas, VARRAYs are bounded and cannot be sparse. It means that VARRAYs have a limit on the number of elements and are bounded; whereas, nested tables do not have a limit on the number of elements and are unbounded. Nested tables can become sparse if elements are deleted; whereas, VARRAYs can never become sparse.

*181. What are implicitly defined records?*

Implicitly defined records are those that do not have the need to describe each field separately in the record definition. The structure of the record is not defined using the TYPE statement; instead, the %ROWTYPE attribute is used to define the implicit record to have the same structure as the database record.

*182. What is a system privilege?*

A system privilege is the right to perform an action in the database. Privileges are granted to a schema. They may be granted to a role, which in turn is granted to schemas.

*183. What is the difference between the create table and create any table privileges?*

The CREATE TABLE privilege grants the schema to create tables in its own schema; however, CREATE ANY TABLE grants the privilege to create any table owned by any other schema as well.

184. What are pseudo-columns? How can you use pseudo columns in procedural statements?

Pseudo columns are not actual columns in a table, but they behave like columns. They are used in SQL statements to retrieve specific information. PL/SQL recognizes pseudo-columns as a part of SQL statements, but they cannot be used directly in a procedural language. The following pseudo-columns are used in SQL:

ROWID

ROWNUM

LEVEL

CURRVAL

NEXTVAL

*185. Can stand-alone programs be overloaded?*

No, stand-alone programs cannot be overloaded; however, packaged sub-programs can be overloaded within the same package.

*186. Can you invoke a stored function or procedure from the oracle forms in the database?*

Yes, a stored procedure or function can be invoked from the Oracle Forms and the result can be used for further programming.

187. What is a SAVEPOINT command?

The SAVEPOINT command is used to set a point within a transaction to which you may rollback. This command helps in cancelling the portions of the current transaction. Using ROLLBACK with the SAVEPOINT TO clause, a transaction can be undone in parts rather than rolling back the entire transaction.

*188. What is a subprogram?*

A named Procedural Language/Structured Query Language (PL/SQL) block is called a subprogram. It has three sections: declarative, executable, and exception handling (optional).

*189. What are the advantages of subprogram?*

The main advantage of a subprogram is that it can be compiled and stored in a database. In addition, it has the following advantages:

Modularization —Refers to a property, which allows you to break the large programs into smaller modules and make the program easy to write and debug.

Easy maintenance —Refers to a property, which allows you to make the modifications in a code because the code is modular and written in one place.

Reusability—Refers to a property, which allows you to reuse the same subprogram within any application. The code of the subprogram need not be re-written each time.

Data integrity and security —Refers to a property, which prevents unauthorized users from accessing the subprogram without the proper rights.

Better performance —Helps in avoiding repeated parsing on subsequent calls to the same subprogram as the code is compiled, parsed, and available in the shared Structured Query Language (SQL) area. This reduces the number of calls to the database; and therefore, increases the network performance.

Code clarity —Allows you to give proper names to the PL/SQL blocks. As a result, the code becomes simpler to understand and gets better clarity.

196. Can a procedure be declared and defined within a PL/SQL block?

Yes, any procedure can be declared and defined within a PL/SQL block.

190. *What is the scope of the procedure defined within a PL/SQL block?*

The scope of any procedure that is defined within the PL/SQL block will be limited as it can be called only within the PL/SQL block and not by any other procedure or calling environment.

191. *What is the difference between create or replace function and drop function commands?*

The CREATE OR REPLACE FUNCTION command creates the function if it does not exist and replaces it with the new version if it already exists. The DROP FUNCTION command deletes the function altogether from the database. Any privilege assigned on the function remains the same when the CREATE OR REPLACE FUNCTION command is used; however, in the case of the DROP FUNCTION command, all the privileges are revoked.

*192. What are function purity levels?*

Function purity levels define what type of data structures can be read or modified by a function. There are four function purity levels, which are given as follows:

WNDS —Writes no database state. The function does not modify any database table using any DML statement.

RNDS—Reads no database state. The function does not read any database tables using the SELECT statement.

WNPS —Writes no package state. The function does not modify any packaged variables.

RNPS— Reads no package state. The function does not read any packaged variables.

*193. Can functions be called as stand-alone programs like procedures?*

No, functions cannot be called as stand-alone programs like procedures. They must be a part of an expression or they should be invoked as part of SQL statements.

## 194. What are the different types of exceptions?

The three types of exceptions that can be handled at runtime are as follows:

Predefined Oracle error —Refers to an undeclared error, which is raised by the Oracle server implicitly.

Non-predefined Oracle error—Refers to an error declared in the declarative section of the code that is raised by the Oracle server implicitly.

User-defined error —Refers to an error declared in the declarative section of the code that is raised explicitly.

## 195. Name few pre-defined Oracle errors ?

Pre-defined Oracle errors are as follows:

NO_DATA_FOUND —Refers to an error when a SELECT statement does not return any result set.

DUP_VAL_ON_INDEX —Refers to an error when a program tries to store duplicate values in an indexed column.

TOO_MANY_ROWS —Refers to an error when a SELECT INTO statement returns more than one row.

VALUE_ERROR —Refers to an error when an arithmetic, conversion, truncation, or size-constraints error occurs.

ROWTYPE_MISMATCH —Refers to an error when the actual and formal parameters do not have the same datatypes

## 196. What happens after a sub-block handles an exception?

When a sub-block handles an exception, the control passes to the next statement in the executable section of the enclosing block immediately after the END statement of the sub-block.

## 197. What is the meaning of pragma keyword?

The PRAGMA keyword signifies that the statement is a compiler directive, which is not processed when the PL/SQL is executed. It is a pseudo-instruction that tells the compiler to interpret all the occurrences of exception name within the block with the associated Oracle server number.

198. What are the steps that a sql statement undergoes for compilation?

SQL statements are compiled using the following steps:

Parse—Refers to a step ,in which statement are checked for existence of all objects used and the syntax is validated.

Bind— Refers to a step ,in which the values for the variables are obtained. This process is also called binding variables.

Execute —Refers to a step, in which the statement is executed by Oracle.

Fetch —Refers to a step, in which rows are selected and retrieved one by one until last row is fetched.

199. What is data independence and why is it important?

Data independence is the ability of to make changes to data characteristics without have to make changes to the programs that access the data. It's important because of the savings in time and potential errors caused by reducing modifications to data access software

200. What is SQL Deadlock?

Deadlock is a unique situation in a multi user system that causes two or more users to wait indefinitely for a locked resource. First user needs a resource locked by the second user and the second user needs a resource locked by the first user. To avoid dead locks, avoid using exclusive table lock and if using, use it in the same sequence and use Commit frequently to release locks.

*201. What is projection?*

The Projection of a relation is defined as projection of all its tuples over a set of attributes. It yields vertical subset of the relation. The projection operation is used to view the number of attributes in the resultant relation or to reorder attributes.

*201. What is Encryption?*

Encryption is the coding or scrambling of data so that humans cannot read them directly.

*202. What is decryption?*

Taking encoded text and converting it into text that you are able to read is called decryption.

*203. What is cardinality?*

The number of instances of each entity involved in an instance of a relation of a relationship describe how often an entity can participate in relationship. (1:1, 1:many, many: many).

205. What is SQL*Loader?

SQL*Loader is a product for moving data in external files into tables in an Oracle database. To load data from external files into an Oracle database, two types of input must be provided to SQL*Loader : the data itself and the control file. The control file describes the data to be loaded. It describes the Names and format of the data files, Specifications for loading data and the Data to be loaded (optional). Invoking the loader sqlload username/password controlfilename <options>.

206. What is Posting?

Posting is an event that writes Inserts, Updates & Deletes in the forms to the database but not committing these transactions to the database.

207. What is Mutating SQL Table?

Mutating Table is a table that is currently being modified by an Insert, Update or Delete statement.

208. What is Synonyms?

Synonyms is the alias name for table, views, sequences & procedures and are created for reasons of Security and Convenience.

*209. What is a Segment?*

A segment is a set of extents allocated for a certain logical structure.

210. What is a Sequence?

A sequence generates a serial list of unique numbers for numerical columns of a database's tables.

Please check this out:

Our other best-selling books

500+ Java & J2EE Interview Questions & Answers-Java & J2EE Programming

200+ Frequently Asked Interview Questions & Answers in iOS Development

200 + Frequently Asked Interview Q & A in SQL , PL/SQL, Database Development & Administration

100+ Frequently Asked Interview Questions & Answers in Scala

100+ Frequently Asked Interview Q & A in Swift Programming

100+ Frequently Asked Interview Q & A in Python Programming

100+ Frequently Asked Interview Questions & Answers in Android Development

100+ most Frequently Asked Interview Questions & Answers in Manual Testing

Frequently asked Interview Q & A in Java programming

Frequently Asked Interview Questions & Answers in J2EE

Frequently asked Interview Q & A in Mobile Testing

Frequently asked Interview Q & A in Test Automation-Selenium Testing

****************************************************

# Please check out our other bestselling books